WITHDRAWN

WITHDRAWN

Welcome to Indonesia

By Patrick Ryan

The Child's World®

Published by The Child's World®
1980 Lookout Drive
Mankato, MN 56003-1705
800-599-READ
www.childsworld.com

Copyright © 2008 The Child's World®
All rights reserved. No part of this book may be
reproduced or utilized in any form or by any means
without written permission from the publisher.
Printed in the United States of America.

Design and Production: The Creative Spark, San Juan Capistrano, CA
Editorial: Emily J. Dolbear, Brookline, MA
Photo Research: Deborah Goodsite, Califon, NJ

Cover and title page: Noboru Komine/Lonely Planet Images
Interior photos: Alamy: 11 (Bruno Barbier/Robert Harding Picture Library Ltd), 14 (Joe Malone/
Jon Arnold Images), 17 (AA World Travel Library), 23 (Peter Treanor); AP Photo: 13 (Binsar Bakkara),
21 (Muchtar Zakaria); Corbis: 6 (Paul C. Pet/zefa), 7 (Mike Alquinto/epa), 3, 19 (Dennis M. Sabangan/epa),
24 (Joson/zefa); Getty Images: 15 (Jason Childs); iStockphoto.com: 28 (Ufuk Zivana), 29, 31 (Erik de
Graaf), 30 (Thomas Gordon); Landov: 26 (Supri/Reuters); Lonely Planet Images: 22 (Paul Beinssen)
25 top (Gregory Adams), 25 bottom (Bernard Napthine); Minden Pictures: 8 (Frans Lanting); NASA
Earth Observatory: 4 (Reto Stockli); Oxford Scientific: 3, 9 (Jtb Photo Communications Inc.), 3, 20
(G & R Maschmeyer/Pacific Stock), 27 (Joe Carini/Pacific Stock); Panos Pictures: 16 (Jan Banning);
Photo Researchers, Inc: 10 (Pascal Goetgheluck).
Map: XNR Productions: 5

Library of Congress Cataloging-in-Publication Data
Ryan, Patrick, 1948–
  Welcome to Indonesia / by Patrick Ryan.
    p. cm. — (Welcome to the world)
  Includes index.
  ISBN-13: 978-1-59296-915-9 (library bound : alk. paper)
  ISBN-10: 1-59296-915-1 (library bound : alk. paper)
  1. Indonesia—Juvenile literature. I. Ryan, Patrick, 1948- Indonesia. II. Title. III. Series.

DS615.R93 2007
959.8—dc22

                    2007005555

Contents

Where Is Indonesia?

If you could fly high up in the air, you would see that Earth is made up of land areas surrounded by water. The seven largest land areas are called **continents**.

The largest continent is Asia. Indonesia (in-doh-NEE-zhuh) is an island country in Southeast Asia. That's the part of Asia that lies south of China and east of India. Indonesia is the biggest country in Southeast Asia in both area and population.

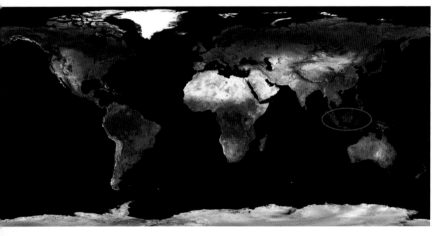

This picture gives us a flat look at Earth.
Indonesia is inside the red circle.

Did you **know?**

Southeast Asia includes the countries of Myanmar, Thailand, Vietnam, Laos, Cambodia, Singapore, Malaysia, Brunei, East Timor, and the Philippines as well as Indonesia.

The Land

Instead of being one piece of land like most countries, Indonesia is made up of many islands. In fact, Indonesia has more than 17,000 islands! The islands stretch for almost 4,000 miles (about 6,400 kilometers) between the Indian and Pacific oceans.

Sulawesi is one of Indonesia's five largest islands.

People live on only about 6,000 of Indonesia's islands. The five largest islands are New Guinea, Borneo, Sumatra, Java, and Sulawesi. Most people in Indonesia live on these islands. Many of Indonesia's islands are very tiny. Most have no people living on them at all.

Did you **know?**

On December 26, 2004, an earthquake in the Indian Ocean set off history's deadliest sea wave, or **tsunami** (soo-NAH-mee). Indonesia suffered the greatest losses (above). The tsunami killed more than 100,000 people and caused billions of dollars of damage in the Aceh province alone. Earthquakes have continued to rock Indonesia, causing even more deaths.

Plants and Animals

A researcher in Indonesia measures a rafflesia.

Rain forests cover many of the islands in Indonesia. There are a variety of trees and wildflowers. You can find the world's largest flower at the famous gardens in Bogor, Indonesia. This plant is called the rafflesia (ruh-FLEE-shuh). It grows up to 3 feet (almost 1 meter) wide and may weigh 20 pounds (9 kilograms)!

Birds and monkeys make their homes in the forests of Indonesia. More rarely there are elephants and rhinoceros. Most of the world's orangutans are found in northern Sumatra and Borneo. Deer, wild pigs, and wild buffalo also live on Indonesia's islands. On the island of Komodo are giant lizards called Komodo dragons. These huge creatures eat the deer and goats that live on the island.

An orangutan clings to its mother in the forests of Borneo.

Long Ago

Very early humans lived on the island of Java more than a million years ago. In 1891, a scientist found the remains

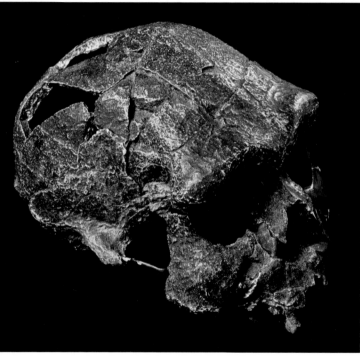

The fossil of the skull of Java man

or trace of past life, or **fossils**, of a human ancestor on the island. This early human, called *Homo erectus*, is known as Java man.

Much later, others came to the island. People formed little kingdoms over time. They moved and spread out to Indonesia's other islands. These kingdoms ruled Indonesia for hundreds of years.

Hindu kings built the ancient Prambanan temples on the island of Java.

After the small kingdoms came to an end, people from Europe ruled Indonesia. These traders thought Indonesia was the perfect stopping place for their ships. They made Indonesians obey new rules they did not like. In the 1600s, the Dutch took control of the area. The Dutch called their **colony** the Netherlands East Indies.

11

Indonesia Today

Indonesians declared independence from the Netherlands on August 17, 1945. But it took four more years to win official independence. The new nation, first called the United States of Indonesia, changed its name to the Republic of Indonesia in 1950.

Conflict over independence in Indonesia continued into the next century. Some groups in the country wanted greater freedom. In 2002, the Indonesian government gave up control of East Timor, an area it had controlled since 1975. The government also signed a peace agreement with those fighting for independence in the Aceh province. Today the people of Indonesia are working hard to remain a united nation.

People in the Aceh province celebrate the signing of a peace treaty with the Indonesian government in 2005.

The People

About 245 million people live in Indonesia. Most Indonesians
are **Muslims**. They follow the teachings of the Islamic
religion. Many Indonesians belong to **ethnic groups**, or
groups of people who share a way of life, language, or race.

**Muslim women with their children
pray in Java.**

Indonesia has the fourth-largest population in the world, after China, India, and the United States. It is also the world's largest Muslim nation.

Even though they may not always understand one another, Indonesians are friendly people. Many like to dance and listen to music. On some islands, men play in gamelan bands for fun. They make gamelan music by striking flat bells called gongs with a padded hammer. Some gamelan bands have more than 50 gongs!

A Balinese gamelan player performs.

15

City Life and Country Life

Jakarta is the capital city of Indonesia. A capital city is where the government of the country works. Jakarta is also one of the world's largest cities, with skyscrapers, shopping malls, super highways, and modern hospitals. People who

A view at night of Jarkarta, Indonesia's capital city

live in Jakarta and other cities usually live in apartments or small houses. City people in Indonesia might work in government or in factories. Or they might make clothes, shoes, electronic goods, and paper products.

In the country, people are used to the old ways of life. Many live in simple huts and villages. They farm their own plots of land. But they also can travel to the cities and are in touch with modern life.

Did you **know?**

In Indonesia's cities, people use the *bajaj* (BAJ-eye) to go places. A bajaj (above) is a three-wheeled motor scooter with space for passengers. Indonesians also travel around the city on motorbikes and by car.

17

Schools and Language

There are many different ethnic groups and languages in Indonesia. That can make teaching difficult. So students are taught in their local language until they reach the third grade. Then they learn the common language of Bahasa Indonesian.

Many children in Indonesia have to leave school to go to work in the fields. This way they can make money and help support their families. For those who are able to finish high school, there are some excellent public universities in Indonesia's cities.

Did you know?

People in Indonesia speak more than 200 languages or variations of languages.

A group of Indonesian schoolchildren have fun after school.

Women in Java planting rice in the fields

Work

Not quite half of the people in Indonesia are farmers. Many grow rice for their families. They also sell rice to other countries. Indonesian farmers also grow and sell rubber, palm oil, peanuts, and coffee. Others work in Indonesia's rain forests. They cut down trees to be used for making furniture and paper. Logging and clearing trees for farmland has threatened the forests, however.

Women are an important part of the economy in Indonesia. They work at all kinds of jobs and have reached the highest offices in government. Megawati Sukarnoputri served as the country's first female president from 2001 to 2004!

Megawati Sukarnoputri

Did you know?

Tourism is a growing business for Indonesia. The island of Bali is a popular vacation spot for people from around the world.

21

Food

People in Indonesia eat vegetables and fish every day, with meat for special occasions. Fruit is plentiful, including papaya, banana, pineapple, star fruit, and coconut. Indonesian food is often spicy. Stews with spices and chilies are common.

Almost everyone in Indonesia likes to eat rice. In fact, people don't consider it a meal without it! Indonesians put many things on top of their rice to make different dishes. Some add spicy beef, crab, or shrimp to their rice. Others like mixed vegetables or fried bananas. On some of the islands, you might even have fresh eel.

A food stall in Bali offers rice with various side dishes.

A merchant sells fish at a traditional street market in the city of Semarang in central Java.

Pastimes

Indonesians play many familiar sports, such as soccer and volleyball. They also have sports of their own. For example, farmers in the eastern islands may hitch two bulls together and race each other. On one island, boys enjoy jumping over

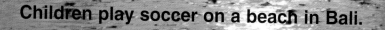

Children play soccer on a beach in Bali.

Traditional Indonesian shadow puppets are called *wayang kulit.*

a high stone. Some other islanders play a board game with shells or pebbles, called *congkak.* People join in and have fun whatever the sport.

At night, many people enjoy attending puppet plays. The puppets are all worked by a performer called a *dalang.* Gamelan players provide music for the shows.

Carved wooden puppets are called *wayang golek.*

Holidays

Muslims in Indonesia observe an important holy month called Ramadan. People **fast**, or do not eat or drink from sunup to sundown, during this time. They break the fast and gather for a feast with special foods after prayers at sundown. Other Indonesians celebrate Christmas and Easter. On Bali, Hindu Indonesians have their own calendar with times of celebration.

Festivals are held on New Year's Day and on Indonesia's Independence Day. Each island has its own local festivals, too.

A 2006 Independence Day festival in Jakarta

26

With its natural beauty and varied culture, Indonesia is a special country. Its people have had to face many challenges. People from around the world still come to see this country. Perhaps one day you will visit the islands of Indonesia, too!

27

Area: 741,000 square miles (1.9 million square kilometers)—about three times the size of Texas

Population: About 245 million people

Capital City: Jakarta

Other Important Cities: Surabaya, Bandung, Medan, and Semarang

Money: The rupiah. One rupiah equals 100 sen, but sen are no longer used.

National Language: Bahasa Indonesia is the official language of Indonesia. Many people also speak English.

National Holiday: Independence Day, August 17 (1945)

Head of Government: The prime minister of Indonesia

Head of State: The president of Indonesia

National Flag: Indonesia's flag has two colors—red and white. The red stands for bravery. The white stands for purity and truth.

Famous People:

Affandi: Javanese painter

Chairil Anwar: poet

Taufik Hidayat: Olympic gold medalist in badminton

Suharto: president of Indonesia from 1967 to 1998

Sukarno: first president of Indonesia, from 1949 to 1966

Megawati Sukarnoputri: first female president of Indonesia from 2001 to 2004

Pramoedya Ananta Toer: award-winning novelist

National Song: "Great Indonesia" (*or "Indonesia Raya"*) W. R. Soepratman wrote the words and music in 1928. It became the national song in 1945.

Indonesia, our native country,
Our birthplace,
Where we all arise to stand
    guard
Over this our Motherland:
Indonesia our nationality,
Our people and our country.
Come then, let us all exclaim
Indonesia united.
Long live our land,
Long live our state,
Our nation, our people,
    and all
Arise then, its spirit,
Arise, its bodies
For Great Indonesia.

CHORUS:
Indonesia the Great,
    independent and free,
Our beloved country.
Indonesia the Great,
    independent and free,
Long live Indonesia the Great!

Indonesia, an eminent
    country,
Our wealthy country,
There we shall be forever.
Indonesia, the country of our
    ancestors,
A relic of all of us.
Let us pray
For Indonesia's prosperity:
May her soil be fertile
And spirited her soul,
The nation and all the people.
Conscious be her heart
And her mind
For Indonesia the Great.
Repeat CHORUS

Indonesia, a sacred country,
Our victorious country:
There we stand
Guarding our true Mother.
Indonesia, a beaming Country,
A country we love with all our
    heart,

Let's make a vow
That Indonesia be there
    forever.
Blessed be her people
And her sons,
All her islands, and her seas.
Fast be the country's progress
And the progress of her youth
For Indonesia the Great.

Repeat CHORUS

29

ENGLISH	INDONESIAN	HOW TO SAY IT
good morning	selamat pagi	suh-lah-maht pah-gy
good-bye	selamat tinggal	suh-lah-maht ting-gall
please	silakan	see-lah-kahn
thank you	terima kasih	teh-ree-muh kah-see
one	satu	sah-too
two	dua	do-uh
three	tiga	tea-gah

colony (KOL-uh-nee) A colony is land that is settled and controlled by people from another country. Indonesia was a colony of the Dutch at one time.

continents (KON-tih-nents) Continents are large areas of land surrounded mostly by water. Indonesia is part of the continent of Asia.

ethnic groups (ETH-nik GROOPS) Ethnic groups are groups of people who share a way of life, language, or race. Indonesia has many different ethnic groups.

fast (FAST) When you fast, you don't eat or drink. During the month of Ramadan, Muslims fast from sunup to sundown.

fossils (FOSS-uhls) Fossils are any remains or trace of past life. Researchers found fossils of early humans in Java, Indonesia.

Muslims (MUHS-lihms) People who follow the teachings of the Islamic religion are called Muslims. Most Indonesians are Muslims.

tsunami (soo-NAH-mee) A tsunami is an enormous sea wave produced by an underwater earthquake or volcano. The 2004 Indian Ocean tsunami was the deadliest in history.

31

Further Information

Read It

Corwin, Jeff. *Into Wild Indonesia*. San Diego: Blackbirch Press, 2004.

Martin, Fred. *Indonesia*. Des Plaines, IL: Heinemann Library, 1998.

Miller, Debra A. *Modern Nations of the World—Indonesia*. San Diego: Lucent Books, 2005.

Torres, John A. *Tsunami Disaster in Indonesia, 2004*. Hockessin, DE: Mitchell Lane Publishers, 2006.

Look It Up

Visit our Web page for lots of links about Indonesia:
http://www.childsworld.com/links

Note to Parents, Teachers, and Librarians: We routinely verify our Web links to make sure they are safe, active sites—so encourage your readers to check them out!

Index

3 1491 00971 5396

Niles
Public Library District
MAY 0 6 2008
Niles, Illinois 60714